Beginning
MOUNTAIN
BIKING

The following athletes were
photographed for this book:
  Lauren Flagg,
  Talisyn Flagg,
  Brian Fuller,
  Jerad Fuller,
  Jason Garza,
  Ryan Gaul,
  Jake Harper,
  Nicole Hektner,
  Kevin Ivy,
  Josh Otzen,
  Mike Tucker.

Beginning
MOUNTAIN
BIKING

Julie Jensen

Adapted from Andy King's
Fundamental Mountain Biking
Photographs by Andy King

Lerner Publications Company ● Minneapolis

The Beginning Sports series was designed in conjunction with the Fundamental Sports series to offer young athletes a basic understanding of various sports at two reading levels.

Library of Congress Cataloging-in-Publication Data

Jensen, Julie, 1957–
   Beginning mountain biking / Julie Jensen ; adapted from Andy King's Fundamental mountain biking ; photographs by Andy King.
      p.   cm.—(Beginning sports)
   Includes bibliographical references and index.
   Summary: Provides information on the history of mountain bicycles and the skills and techniques, competitions, and fancy tricks involved in riding them.
      ISBN 0-8225-3509-2 (alk. paper)
   1. All terrain cycling—Juvenile literature. [1. All terrain cycling.] I. King, Andy. Fundamental mountain biking II. Title. III. Series.
GV1056.J46   1997
796.6'4—dc20   96-20941

Manufactured in the United States of America
1 2 3 4 5 6 – JR – 01 00 99 98 97 96

Photo Acknowledgments
Photos reproduced with permission of: pp. 8,10 (both), © Wende Cragg; p. 9, Haynes Foundation Collection, Montana Historical Society; p. 33, Courtesy GT Bicycles; p. 35 (top left), © Nathan Bilow, Courtesy Fat Tire Bike Week; p. 35 (top right), © Xani Fané, Courtesy Fat Tire Bike Week; pp. 42, 62, Courtesy Cannondale Corporation.

Diagram on p. 14 courtesy of *All Action Mountain Biking,* by Bob Allen, published by Wayland Publishers Limited. All other diagrams and artwork by Laura Westlund.

Contents

Chapter 1

HOW THIS SPORT GOT STARTED

Would you like to fly through a forest like an owl? Would you like to be able to go wherever you wanted to, not just where the path goes? On a mountain bike, you can!

Bicycles have always meant freedom to people. Bicycles help people get to places faster than they would by walking. Bicycles help people go places they couldn't get to on foot.

Bicycles were first created in the early 1800s. These bicycles were awkward and hard to control. Mechanics kept improving the design of bicycles. By about 1890, people could ride bicycles with air-filled tires and handlebars that moved.

7

"Repack" is the name of a hill in Marin County, California. In the 1970s, mountain bike racing first became popular on this hill, which drops 1,300 feet in less than 2 miles. Riders had to repack, or replace, the grease that sizzled out of the coaster brakes after lunging down this steep hill. Coaster brakes are brakes that stop a bike when the rider pedals backward. The hill became known as "Repack" to those who rode it. The last Repack race was run in 1984.

Most people in the 1890s used bicycles for entertainment or for moving around in towns. Some military leaders thought bikes would be a good way to move soldiers quickly on battlefields. The U.S. Army formed the Twenty-fifth Bicycle Corps Regiment in the late 1890s. The soldiers rode sturdy metal bikes that weighed 90 pounds.

Once, in June 1897, the soldiers rode their bikes from their base in Missoula, Montana, to St. Louis, Missouri. Although the bikes and riders completed the 1,900-mile test, the Army never used bicycles very much.

To the Hills

In the 1950s, John Finley Scott wanted to ride on mountain trails in Oregon and California. Scott began tinkering with his bike so he could ride off-road. He put **balloon tires** on his bike and added **gears**.

Not many other people wanted to ride Scott's bikes in the 1950s. But in the 1970s, bicyclists began racing down the hills in northern California.

Members of the Twenty-fifth Bicycle Corps of the U.S. Army climb a hill in Montana in 1896.

Regular bikes didn't work very well for them. So they made their own bikes, called "clunkers," with parts of other bikes.

Some hills were too steep to ride. The riders had to push their bikes up the hill. When they rode downhill, grease ran out of the bikes' **brakes.** Grease kept the metal pieces in the brakes from rubbing against each other. When a rider went fast and then tried to stop, the grease melted.

Above, Joe Breeze, left, and Charlie Kelly were some of the first bicyclists to take their bikes off the regular paths. Below, Kelly heads down Repack Hill.

Gary Fisher, Charlie Kelly, Joe Breeze, Tom Ritchey, Wende Cragg, and others kept working on their bikes. They used **fat tires** with deep treads for good **traction** on the steep hills. They made a bike **frame** that was sturdy enough to last many rough rides. They built better brake and gear systems. They flattened the bike's handlebars for better control. They transformed a clunker into a "mountain bike."

Modern Bikes

By 1981, companies were making and selling mountain bikes. By 1996, mountain biking was so popular that it became an exhibition sport in the Summer Olympic Games.

Modern mountain bikes are made of strong, light metals such as aluminum, steel, and titanium. A bike often weighs less than 25 pounds and has a set of springs to absorb bumps.

Many mountain bikers never ride off paved roads. But if you want to go off-road, this book will show you how to do just that. And mountain biking off-road is a whole new sport!

Chapter 2

BASICS

Equipment

You could ride most bicycles off-road, but many street bikes would be damaged by the rough ride. If you're riding off-road, use a mountain bike.

All mountain bikes have the same basic parts. First, a mountain bike has a strong frame. The frame must be able to stand up to the bumps and jolts of the road—and occasional spills.

A mountain bike's tires are wider than regular street bike tires. These tires are called fat tires, or knobbies. A knobby has rubber bumps on its deep tread. The bumps give the bike traction. Fat tires make the bike more stable, and they don't get as many holes as regular tires do.

Mountain bike tires have deep, knobby treads. The tires come in various colors with different tread patterns.

13

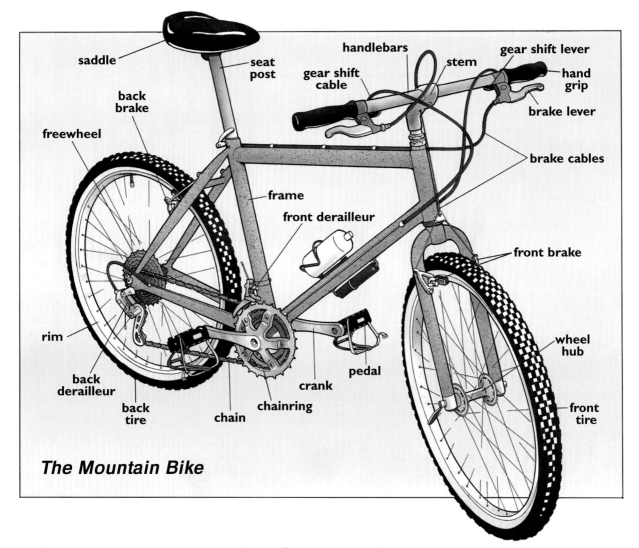

saddle

seat post

back brake

freewheel

handlebars

gear shift cable

stem

gear shift lever

hand grip

brake lever

brake cables

frame

front derailleur

front brake

rim

front brake

back derailleur

wheel hub

back tire

back tire

chain

chainring

crank

pedal

front tire

The Mountain Bike

A mountain bike has 15 to 21 gears. Other bikes have 10 or fewer gears. The extra gears help riders pedal up hills.

A bike's chain goes around a chainring and a freewheel. The chainring is connected to the pedal **cranks.** When you pedal, the chainring turns the chain. When the chain moves, it turns the freewheel, which turns the rear wheel.

The chainring and freewheel have sprockets, or toothed wheels, of different sizes. The number of gears your bike has depends on the number of sprockets it has.

The gear shift lever on the right side of the handlebars

connects to the back **derailleur** (dih-RAY-luhr), or gear-switching operation. The gear shift lever on the left controls the front derailleur. When you move the chain to different sprockets, you change the gear you are in.

When the chain is on a large sprocket in front and a small freewheel track in back, the bike is in a high gear. One turn of the pedals will turn the rear wheel about three times. That moves the bike about 21 feet. High gears are for speed on flat ground!

When climbing a hill, the rider shifts the chain to a smaller sprocket on the front and a larger sprocket on the freewheel. This puts the bike into a lower gear. In a low gear, one turn of the pedal turns the rear wheel only once. The bike moves about 7 feet.

The Derailleur

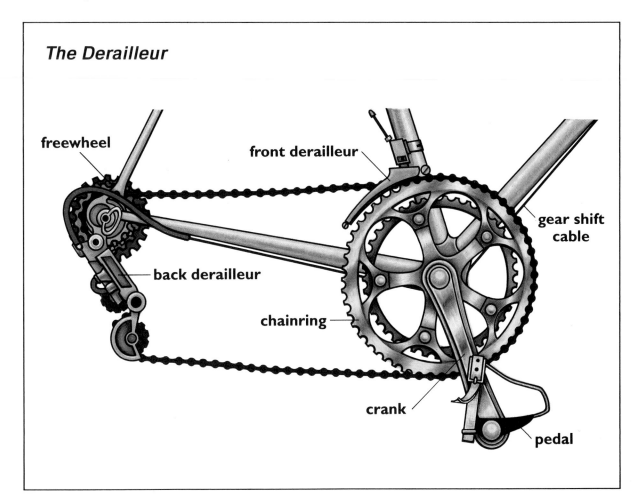

freewheel

front derailleur

gear shift cable

back derailleur

chainring

crank

pedal

As the riders above show, bike gloves and helmets come in all sorts of styles and colors.

Bike shop owners can straighten, or "true," a wheel for you if one is bent out of shape.

The brake levers are also on the handlebars. The back brake lever is on the right side. The front brake lever is on the left.

Brakes stop a bike by keeping the wheels from turning. There are two brake pads on each wheel, one on each side of the wheel. When you squeeze a brake lever, the pads clamp against the wheel.

The brake pads will slow the wheel if you squeeze lightly. If you squeeze hard, the pads will stop the wheel.

● Getting Fit

Mountain bikes cost from $200 to thousands of dollars. Be sure a bike fits you before you buy one. Here's one way to tell if a bike is the right size. Stand with one leg on each side of the bike. There should be about 2 to 4 inches of room between you and the bike. Then sit on the bike's **saddle**, or seat. (You may need to have someone hold the bike while you're sitting on it.) The seat of a mountain bike is set farther back than the seat of a street bike. Be sure you can reach the gear shift lever and the brake lever on each side. Your feet should rest on the pedals with your knees slightly bent.

● What to Wear

It's a good idea to wear a helmet whenever you ride a bike. Wearing a helmet is even more important when you're riding off-road because your chances of crashing are much greater. Helmets are made of foam and hard plastic. Get a helmet that meets safety standards. Get a new helmet if yours cracks.

Pedal Power

*Your pedals drive your bike. You want to pull up the pedals while pedaling, as well as push them down. Two items of equipment—**toeclips** and clipless pedals can help.*

Toeclips are shown in the photo above. Toeclips hold your feet on the pedals with a cage around your toes. You can easily pull out your feet if you need to touch the ground. You can wear any kind of shoes with toeclips.

Clipless pedals come with matching shoes. The photo below shows a clipless shoe and pedal. The pedal and shoe have latches. You attach and remove the shoe by twisting your foot.

Trail Safety

Here are some rules of the trail that will help you have a safe and fun ride.
1. *Only ride on open trails on which bikes are allowed.*
2. *Don't litter.*
3. *Ride so that you can control your bike. This protects you and others on the trail.*
4. *Be nice to hikers and other bikers. Say "Hi" or ring your bike's bell to let them know you're coming.*
5. *Never spook animals. When passing horses or encountering wildlife, slow down.*
6. *Think ahead. Be sure you have the right equipment for the trail you're riding. Make sure you can handle any challenge the path presents.*
7. *Wear a helmet.*
8. *Watch the weather. Don't get caught in the rain.*

Wearing glasses or goggles will protect your eyes. Padded gloves will make gripping the handlebars easier.

Where to Ride

You can ride a mountain bike almost anywhere. Many local and state parks have trails for biking. In some states, mountain bikers can ride on ski slopes during the summer.

Let's follow Josh and Ryan on their mountain bike ride. They start at Josh's house. First, they check their tires. They look over their bikes for any problems. Then they put on their helmets and take off.

Josh and Ryan begin their ride on their neighborhood streets. They watch for traffic and obey the traffic signs. Soon they reach a park trail. It's time to go off-road!

The dirt path is not smooth like the street. Josh and Ryan keep their arms slightly bent as they pedal. They're ready to lift themselves off their seats if they hit any bumps.

Ryan leads the way down the path through the trees. There's a sharp right turn ahead. Ryan shifts his weight and uses his brakes as he leans into the turn. Next, Ryan and Josh head left. They go down a small hill. There are rocks at the bottom. The boys use their brakes again as they ride over the small rocks.

When the trail turns left and goes up a hill, both boys groan. They pedal fast to pick up speed before they start up the hill. When Ryan's pedaling slows, he shifts gears. He can pedal more easily in the lower gear. Josh shifts down, too. The hill is very steep. By the time Ryan and Josh reach the crest of the hill, their hearts are pounding. Then Josh and Ryan head down the hill. They pick up speed as they go, until they are nearly flying.

Fixing a Flat

You will have to do some repair work on your mountain bike. For most bikes, you need special tools to work on the cranks, **wheel hubs,** and **spokes.** A bike shop can do any tricky fixes, but the most common problem is a flat tire. Fortunately, a flat is easy to fix.

First, you will need the tools pictured above: prying bars for taking off the tire, a tube patch kit, and a pump. Bike stores sell prying bars, pumps, and patch kits. These kits contain glue and a patch.

To change a tire, first open the tire valve. The valve is attached to your tire and sticks up through the rim. Press down on the valve stem to push out any air.

Slide your prying tools between the rim and the tire on either side of the valve. Pry the tire back and up over the edge of the rim. Once you have the tire over the rim, keep pulling one side of the tire out over the rim. Push the valve out through the hole in the rim.

Find the leak in the tube. If you can't see it, pump air into the tire and listen for air leaking. If you can't hear the leak, dunk the tire in water and look for bubbles. Once you find the leak, mark the spot clearly. Let the air out of the tire again.

Clean the surface of the tire. Then scrape it with a roughing tool. Sometimes the leak will be hard to spot after this step so be sure to mark it clearly. Put the glue on an area larger than your patch. Most glues must dry a little, until the area feels sticky, before you can put on the patch. Remove the backing from the patch and put it on the area. Press evenly on the patch. Hold it down for a minute or more.

Put the valve through the rim. Insert the tube around the whole tire. Pull the tire over the rim. Use the prying bars to pry the tire over the edge of the rim.

Once the tire is on the wheel, pump it up about a third full. Push the side of the tire to make sure the tube is not twisted or off-center inside the tire. Then fill the tire to the correct pressure.

Chapter 3

MANEUVERS

Do you already know how to ride a bicycle? That's a good start, but riding off-road will take some new skills. You will need to know how to turn on rough roads and use your brakes when riding downhill. Mountain bikers need to stay in complete control of their bikes.

Balancing

Talisyn, shown at right, knows that pedaling fast will help her keep her balance. The faster she moves, the less likely she is to tip. When she starts out, Talisyn shifts her weight slightly. She turns the handlebars to balance herself. Once she is going faster, her forward **momentum** will help her stay balanced.

Steering

Some turns are "natural." Others are "forced." A natural turn is made over a long distance. A forced turn is done more quickly.

Lauren, shown on these two pages, is making a natural

turn. As Lauren begins to make a lefthand turn, she leans left, into the turn. By doing this, she changes the position of her bike. Lauren is moving slowly, so she doesn't lean much. She just shifts her weight slightly to change direction. If Lauren did not lean, the force of the turn would push her body away from the direction she wanted to go. She might fall.

As Lauren feels the bike shift, she turns the handlebars to the left to complete the turn. Lauren is moving slowly, so she turns the handlebars just a little. Then, she moves them back to the center position. She shifts her weight so that it's balanced over the bike.

When Lauren turns to the right, she does the same thing except she leans to the right. As Lauren's speed increases, her lean must also. When she goes through a fast turn, she leans more. Leaning helps Lauren counter the forces of gravity that pull her away from the direction of the turn.

On these two pages, Lauren is doing a forced turn. She turns her handlebars quickly to go around the log. She doesn't have to lean much because the turn is done quickly.

Braking

Your right hand controls the rear brake. Your left hand controls the front brake. The front brake is stronger than the back brake. If you squeeze the brake levers lightly, the brakes will slow the wheels. Use a firmer squeeze to stop. How you use your brakes depends on the situation. But braking should always be done smoothly.

In the photos at left, Kevin is using his brakes on level ground. If Kevin brakes only with his front brake, his front tire will slow down but the rear tire won't. Kevin's momentum will push him forward, over the handlebars. He might crash. If Kevin squeezes only the rear brake, the rear tire will slow down but the front tire won't. If that happens, the rear tire might **fishtail,** or swing from side to side. To brake smoothly, Kevin squeezes both brake levers evenly.

Mike, shown on the next page, brakes while going downhill. Mike stays low. He keeps his weight back over his back wheel.

Mike can control his bike better when his tires are rolling than when they are sliding. He lightly squeezes his brakes and releases them. This is called **feathering. Skidding** at the bottom is fun, but skidding with knobby tires damages the trail. To keep trails in good shape, don't skid.

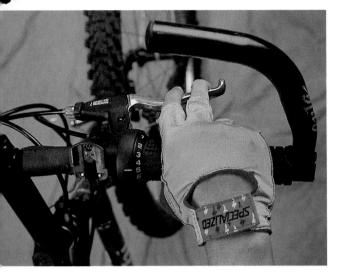

The shifter in the photo above is a grip shifter. To shift gears with this type of shifter, you turn the knob to the number of the gear you want to use. The brake lever is in front of the handlebar. The shifter in the photo below is a thumb shifter. To shift gears with this type of shifter, you move the small lever with your thumb. The brake lever is again in front of the handlebars.

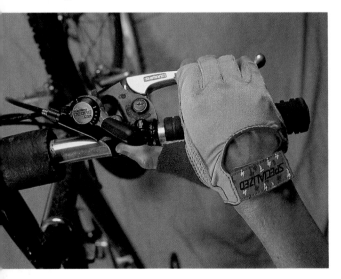

Pedaling and Gears

Your bike "runs" on your pedaling power. Gears help you use this power. Low gears make it easy for you to turn the pedals. In low gear, you can pedal very fast. This makes riding up hills easier. High gears make it hard for you to turn the pedals, but each turn provides more power. In a high gear, you may have to push too hard. High gears are for going fast!

As you come to a hill, shift to a lower gear. You will keep your balance if you **spin,** or pedal continuously, when you shift. While you're still on the flat section, use your left shifter. This will move the front chainring to a smaller sprocket. Still pedaling, use your right hand to shift the freewheel to a larger sprocket. You will be able to pedal faster in the lower gear. Even if the hill is steep, you will be able to pedal fast enough to keep your balance as you go up the hill.

Shifting gears takes practice. As you ride your mountain bike, you'll learn how to use all the gears.

Putting It All Together

The more you ride, the more comfortable you will feel while balancing, turning, and braking. Think about when you are running. If you want to run faster, you think about going faster. Then your legs start moving faster. You can do the same thing when riding on your mountain bike.

Chapter 4

COMPETITION

Many riders enjoy riding in mountain bike races. There's more than one kind of off-road race. There are downhill, uphill, and cross-country races. There's also a competitive event called observed trials.

The National Off-Road Bicycle Association (NORBA) runs off-road races. NORBA is part of the United States Cycling Federation. NORBA began in 1983. It sets rules and standards for races. World championships are held in the United States and Europe. More races are being held around the country every year. Look for information about races in newspapers or at bike shops in your area.

Downhill racers follow a course that usually starts at the top of a hill. The racers ride through a series of gates. Flags

Off-Road Champ!

Juliana Furtado was born in New York City, but she feels at home on dirt trails. Juli is a professional mountain biker. She began racing on street bicycles. Then, in 1989, she switched to mountain bikes. By 1995, Juli had won four cross-country World Cup championships and six cross-country national championships.

33

or plastic poles mark the gates. In some downhill races, called "time trials," a racer is timed as he or she rides the course alone. The racer with the fastest time wins. In a slalom race, two racers ride at the same time on side-by-side courses. Racers need steady nerves and a sturdy bike for this race. The first racer to finish the course wins.

A mountain biker needs strength and endurance to race on an uphill course. The first racer to climb the hill wins the uphill race.

Cross-country racers follow a course. The course can be in the shape of a circle, or it can go from one point to another. A cross-country race is often the main event during a festival. Beginning riders ride short cross-country races. Advanced and professional riders race from 10 to 100 miles.

Riders need skill, not speed, to win in observed trials. Riders must ride over and around a course full of rocks and logs. The riders try not to touch a foot to the ground because they lose points if they do.

More Ways to Ride

Your mountain bike can be a fun way for you to get to school. Here are some other uses for a mountain bike.

***Bicycle polo, above:** Bicycle polo players ride bikes instead of horses. They hit a ball with mallets on a grass field.*

***Bicycle limbo, top right:** Riders ride a bike under a pole that is lowered, little by little.*

***Bike cops, right:** Police officers in many large cities regularly patrol on mountain bikes.*

***Mountain bike tours:** A mountain bike vacation is a great way to see other parts of the country. Popular vacation spots are found in Utah, Colorado, and California.*

The Race

Let's follow Jason as he rides in a cross-country race. He saw a flyer about the race in a bike shop. Jason has been training for several months, and he wants to test himself. He's going to ride in the first race of the day. It's a two-lap race, so he'll ride nearly five miles.

When Jason arrives at the course, he pays the entry fee. He gets a number, which he puts on the front of his bike. The racers will start the race in groups, or heats. The race starter calls the riders to the line by number. Soon, Jason's group is called to take the course.

The race begins. As the riders spread out, Jason speeds up for the first **straightaway.** Then the

course goes into the trees. Jason makes the tight turns and jumps the roots on the path.

Coming out of the trees, Jason sees a short downhill stretch that leads to another hill. He pedals hard to climb the hill. Sweat runs down his neck. Jason feels his heart pound. He struggles to keep his legs pumping.

When Jason rounds the next corner, a few fans cheer for him. During a flat stretch, Jason grabs his water bottle. He takes a quick drink. The cheers and the water give him more energy.

The course turns and heads up a steep, rocky hill. Jason leans back on his bike and pumps his legs. He pulls up on his handlebars to jump a large root. Turning a corner, he brushes against a tree.

Jason's training is paying off as he heads into the last lap. He feels good. Jason zooms through the trees. He starts up the last big hill before the finish line. His legs start to feel like rubber, but he keeps going.

When Jason is almost at the top, he slows down too much. He has to push his bike up the last few feet. Then he jumps back on his bike.

Jason looks ahead. He can see the finish line. He wants to finish the race strong so he pushes hard. Jason finishes in fourth place in his age group. His mom and brother congratulate him as he takes a long drink of water.

You might not always win the race, but you can have other victories. Making it to the top of a steep hill is a victory. So is going faster than your previous time. These personal victories, and the fun of riding with others, make off-road racing fun.

Chapter 5

PRACTICE, PRACTICE

The best way to become a good mountain biker is also the most fun—ride! To be a good rider, you need endurance, strength, and skill. Riding your mountain bike as often as you can will help you develop all these areas.

Stretch before every ride to keep your muscles loose and to prevent injuries. Maybe you will get some training ideas from the following routines of Jerad, Brian, Kevin, and Lauren.

Endurance Training

Jerad and Brian, at right, are building their endurance. They want to be able to ride for at least an hour without becoming tired and out of breath. To train for endurance, they take long rides on paved roads.

41

From BMX to Mountains

Tinker Juarez began learning off-road bike skills when he rode in bicycle moto-cross (BMX) events near his home in Los Angeles. Tinker was a very good BMX rider. Then, when he was 28 years old, Tinker became a professional mountain bike racer.

Tinker is one of the top mountain bike racers in the world. In 1994, Tinker was the silver medalist in the World Cross-Country Championships. In 1995, he won a gold medal at the Pan American Games and he was the NORBA national champion.

When riding on roads, Jerad and Brian can keep pedaling at a constant and steady pace. Off-road riding is more fun, but it requires quick bursts of energy. Long, steady pedaling builds endurance.

Jerad and Brian started their training by riding for 45 minutes without stopping. They try to ride a little longer each week.

Strength Training

Kevin is training for strength. First, he stretches. Then he warms up by riding for several minutes. After the warm-up, Kevin is ready to ride a steep hill. As he starts to climb, he practices shifting gears. Kevin keeps his pedals spinning as he cranks to the top of the hill. Once at the top, he turns around and goes down. Kevin climbs the hill several times.

Training on hills is hard. Start slowly. Ride up the hill two or three times. As you become stronger, try to climb the hill more times. Climbing hills will make you stronger. You'll also be able to practice shifting.

Using a low gear will make climbing the hill easier. But when you're using a low gear, your back tire spins faster. To keep a good grip on the path, you need to keep weight on the back tire. In the photo on this page, Kevin sits on his saddle. That keeps his weight over the back tire.

Kevin might not be able to make it up the hill by staying in his seat. He might have to stand on his pedals to get more power. Even when Kevin is standing, he keeps his weight back so that the back tire doesn't lose traction. Kevin also pulls up on the handlebars to shift weight to the back.

Bike-Handling Skills

When you're out riding, look for a path with trees and many tight turns. Maybe you can even find a log or two. You can practice shifting, balancing, braking, and steering on these paths. This will sharpen your bike-handling skills.

Lauren, above, has found a challenging path. She has to go over a log in her path. Lauren pulls on her handlebars to raise her front tire. As her front tire starts over the log, Lauren shifts her weight forward. Her back tire rolls over the log.

Your Routine

Every time you ride your mountain bike, you gain experience. This experience will help you find your own way of training. You may want to end a long ride with a few trips up hills. Or you may decide to work on just one skill during each long ride. The more you ride your bike, the more comfortable you will feel on it and the better rider you will be.

RAZZLE DAZZLE

Do you want to ride in observed trials? If you do, you'll have to learn how to hop up and over logs, large rocks, and other obstacles. Observed trials riders master some of the most challenging courses in mountain biking.

Even if you don't want to be an observed trials rider, you can learn some tricks. These moves will help you control your bike on any surface.

Balancing

It's easy to balance your bike while you're moving. But balancing when you aren't moving can be hard.

Talisyn, at right, is standing on her pedals. Her weight is centered over the bike. She keeps her balance by quickly turning her handlebars right or left. At first, practice this move when you're going very slowly. Soon, you'll be able to stay balanced without moving.

49

Hopping

To jump over a log, you have to be able to **hop.** Jerad shows how to do this important—and flashy—skill.

Jerad rides at medium speed toward the log. Right before he gets to the log, he stands on the pedals. At the same time, he pulls up on the handlebars. This motion pulls his front wheel up and over the log.

Then he leans forward and pulls up on his pedals. This lifts the back of the bike up and over the log. The back tire then rolls down the back of the log.

Once you know how to hop, you'll be hopping many times on tough mountain courses. You can also hop up on curbs while riding on a street.

Catching Air

Riding over a bump so fast that your bike leaves the ground is called "catching air." This is one of the most exciting moves in mountain biking. It is also a dangerous move. Before you catch air, make sure the spot you're going to land on doesn't have any rocks or logs on it. If you fall while catching air, try to push your bike away from you. The sharp edges on the bike could hurt you. Of course, you can't always push your bike away as you fall. That's one reason a smart mountain biker always wears a helmet.

Let's see how Jason catches air. He is pedaling fast down a trail. As Jason comes to a bump in the path, he stands up on his pedals. Jason keeps his body low and close to the bike. He bends his arms as he rises over the bump. Jason stays centered over his pedals. As Jason rises, he pulls slightly on his handlebars to raise his front tire. He lands on his rear tire, which gives him better balance.

Walk and Carry

Sometimes, you just can't make it up a hill. Some hills are too steep. And sometimes, you won't want to ride your bike down a hill. In these cases, you can carry or walk your bike.

Talisyn, in the photos on this page, shows how to **dismount** while the bike is still moving. She swings her right leg over the bike and jumps to the ground on both feet. When she's off the bike, she grabs it in the middle of the top bar.

She picks up the bike and puts it on her right shoulder. She holds onto the handlebars as she carries the bike.

Nicole, above, is walking her bike up a hill. After Nicole dismounts, she puts her left hand on the seat and her right hand on the handlebars. She pushes the bike up the hill. If it's a very steep or slippery hill, Nicole uses the bike for support.

Off-Road Training Log

Are you training for a race? Do you ride just for fun? Either way, you can keep track of your progress as a rider by keeping a record of your rides.

If you plan to race, or if you just want to get better, set up a routine. For instance, your schedule might look like this:

> **Monday:** *rest*
> **Tuesday:** *fast ride with some hill climbing to build strength*
> **Wednesday:** *slow ride to practice skills*
> **Thursday:** *a long road ride, maybe with a friend*
> **Friday:** *rest or a slow ride*
> **Saturday:** *long endurance ride, maybe for a few hours*
> **Sunday:** *slow ride with friends*

Try different routines until you find one you like. Then, keep a log of your rides. This will show you how you've improved. You can keep a log of your rides even if you don't set up a training schedule. A log will help you remember cool trails you found. Items you might write in your log are:

- *Distance*
- *Time*
- *Heart rate*
- *Skills you worked on*
- *Weather and how you handled it*
- *How your bike worked*
- *Any repairs your bike needs*
- *What you saw*
- *Where you went*
- *How you felt*

Handling Ditches

A small stream or ditch can be a problem for a rider. Be ready to do the move Jake is doing in the photos on the previous page and this page.

As Jake starts down into the ditch, he shifts his weight back. When he hits the bottom, he bends lower. To climb the other side of the ditch, he pulls up on the handlebars. This puts more weight on his back tire and gives him better traction.

Dirt, Rocks, and Sand

Off-road trails can be made of dirt, rocks, gravel, or sand. Or, a trail can have some of each of these surfaces.

You will get the best traction on a trail if it's dry packed dirt. Don't ride on dirt trails right after a rain. Riding on wet trails will leave ruts. This will hurt the trail by speeding up erosion.

If you're riding on gravel, be ready for your tires to slip when you pedal hard uphill or go around corners. Keep your weight back on the bike. Try not to turn on gravel. If you have to turn, drag your foot on the ground so that you don't fall.

It's a good idea to avoid big rocks. Riding on them can knock you off balance. If you ride on a solid-rock area, be careful. You won't have any problem controlling your bike, but your tires could get caught in a crack.

There's often sand at the bottom of hills. It's tough to control a bike on sand. Try riding straight ahead. Don't stop pedaling until you're out of the sand.

Mountain biking is a great way to explore. No matter how many times you ride over a trail, no two rides will ever be the same. On a mountain bike, every ride is an adventure.

BIKE TALK

balloon tires: Wide, flexible tires that provide a soft, cushioned ride.

brakes: Devices to stop or slow a bike by keeping the wheels from turning.

cranks: The pieces of metal that attach the pedals to the chainring.

derailleur: The mechanism that moves the chain from one sprocket to another. The front derailleur moves the chain on the chainwheel, and the rear derailleur moves the chain on the freewheel. The term is French, from "to take off the rail."

dismount: The act of getting off a bike.

fat tires: Wide bike tires with deep treads.

feathering: Lightly squeezing and releasing the brakes in order to control the bike's speed.

fishtail: To swing out to one side and slide in an arc. The bike's back tire sometimes fishtails while a rider is braking, especially if the braking is fast and hard.

frame: The basic metal structure of the bike.

gears: The system of controls used to make pedaling easier or harder by moving the chain from one set of sprockets to another.

hop: To raise a bike off the ground and over an obstacle.

momentum: The force of movement of an object in one direction.

saddle: The seat of the bike.

skidding: Scraping the tires on a surface by suddenly braking.

spin: To pedal rapidly to keep up speed.

spokes: Slender metal bars that support the rim of the wheel.

straightaway: A direct course, or part of a course, that doesn't turn.

toeclips: The cage-like pieces of equipment that hold a rider's feet to the pedals while riding.

traction: The friction that keeps bike tires from slipping on a surface.

wheel hubs: The metal parts that hold spokes to the center of a wheel.

FURTHER READING

Abramowski, Dwain. *Mountain Bikes.* New York: Franklin Watts, 1990.

Allen, Bob. *Mountain Biking.* Minneapolis: Lerner Publications, 1992.

Gould, Tim and Simon Burney. *Mountain Bike Racing.* San Francisco: Bicycle Books, 1992.

Van der Plas, Robert. *Mountain Bike Book.* San Francisco: Bicycle Books, 1994.

Van der Plas, Robert. *Mountain Bike Magic.* San Francisco: Bicycle Books, 1991.

Woodward, Bob. *Sports Illustrated Mountain Biking: The Complete Guide.* New York: Sports Illustrated Winner's Circle Books, 1990.

FOR MORE INFORMATION

International Mountain Bike
   Association (IMBA)
Route 2, Box 303
Bishop, CA 93514

National Off-Road Bicycle Association
   (NORBA)
P.O. Box 1901
Chandler, AZ 85244

Missy Giove is an exciting rider on the women's mountain bike circuit.

INDEX